Peru's MRTA

Tupac Amarú Revolutionary Movement

Suzie Baer

The Rosen Publishing Group, Inc.
New York

For Tom and Stefan for their love and support

Published in 2003 by The Rosen Publishing Group, Inc.
29 East 21st Street, New York, NY 10010

First Edition

Library of Congress Cataloging-in-Publication Data

Baer, Suzie.
Peru's MRTA : Tupac Amarú Revolutionary Movement / Suzie Baer.
  p. cm. — (Inside the world's most infamous terrorist organizations)
Summary: Discusses the origins, philosophy, and most notorious attacks of the Túpac Amaru terrorist group, including their present activities, possible plans, and counter-terrorism efforts directed against them.
Includes bibliographical references and index.
ISBN 0-8239-3824-7
1. Movimiento Revolucionario Túpac Amaru—History. 2. Terrorism—Peru—History—20th century. 3. Violence—Peru—History—20th century. 4. Berenson, Lori. 5. Prisoners, Foreign—Peru. [1. Túpac Amaru Revolutionary Movement. 2. Terrorism—Peru. 3. Berenson, Lori. 4. Political prisoners. 5. Peru—History—1980– .]
I. Title. II. Series.
HV6433.P42M6817 2002
985.06'4—dc21

2002010600

Contents

Introduction

The Tupac Amarú Revolutionary Movement (in Spanish, Movimiento Revolucionario Tupac Amarú, or MRTA) was formed in 1983 by university student radicals Nestor Cerpa, Victor Polay, and Miguel Rincon to fight corruption in the Peruvian government. The name of the movement came from a famous Incan warrior, Tupac Amarú, who, in the 1570s, fought against the Spaniards who had conquered the Inca Empire. Tupac Amarú was defeated in this war and was executed. His name lived on, however, and in the 1780s, another native Indian group fighting against oppressive leaders named themselves Tupac Amarú II. This group was also defeated, and its leaders were executed.

The stated goal of the MRTA was to reform the Peruvian government and create a new society in which all the people were treated equally, enjoyed the same opportunities and level of prosperity, and shared ownership of all property (including land, schools, companies, and factories). Cerpa, Polay, and Rincon wanted to start their own political party, one that was not dependent on money from the outside world, specifically the United States. When money is lent from one government to another, the donor country often puts restrictions on the government that accepts the loan, forcing it to adopt certain economic

This is an undated photo of Nestor Cerpa, one of the three founding members of the MRTA and its military commander. Unlike other MRTA leaders who came from the middle class, Cerpa (also known as Commandante Evaristo) was from a working-class family and was active in the Peruvian labor movement of the 1970s. As a young trade union official in 1978, Cerpa and his fellow workers took control of a bankrupt textile factory near Lima after its owners tried to close it down. Four people died in the conflict, and Cerpa served a year in prison.

Miguel Rincon *(center)*, the MRTA's second-in-command, is escorted by police following his capture on December 1, 1995, after an armed standoff in a wealthy neighborhood of Lima. As he was led away, Rincon shouted, "My capture is a blow to the MRTA, but the MRTA does not depend on one or two persons."

and political policies. The MRTA felt that these restrictions were put in place to benefit foreign countries and wealthy, influential Peruvians, but not the poor. The MRTA did not trust the motives of its government and wanted to serve the Peruvian people fairly and justly.

Like its namesakes, the MRTA was at war with what it considered to be an oppressive power—the Peruvian government. MRTA members decided that the best way to fight this war was to attack—with nonlethal force—people and organizations that had power and money. They felt that only by targeting the powerful could they get the government's—and the world's—attention and expose the Peruvian government's corruption and human-rights violations for all to see. Members of the Peruvian government, including the president, were long suspected of bribing judges and politicians, stealing money from the government treasury for personal use, trafficking drugs and weapons, and mistreating and murdering political opponents and prisoners. This misuse of government funds and suppression of democracy helped to insure that wealthy citizens would only get wealthier, while the vast majority of poor Peruvians would not get the help that they desperately needed.

The element that set the MRTA apart from most other terrorist organizations was its commitment to the avoidance of unnecessary violence. The group's members felt that the harming of civilians—even members of the social and political elite—was wrong. Throughout most of its history, the MRTA sought to avoid violence whenever possible. However, this respect for human life would not save the group from a violent end.

The Birth of the MRTA

In 1533, the Spanish explorer Francisco Pizarro conquered the Incas and took control of Peru in the name of the Spanish Empire. The coastal city of Lima, founded by Pizarro in 1535, became Peru's capital, and the country turned out to be an important and prestigious acquisition for Spain. Eventually, Peruvian colonists wanted to gain independence from Spain, which had no interest in losing a valuable colony. After several hundred years of fighting, Peru won its independence on July 28, 1821.

Independence, however, did not bring democracy and freedom for all. Since overthrowing Spanish rule, the Peruvian government has repeatedly swung back and forth between civil government (run by civilian representatives of the country's citizens) and military dictatorship (run by one member of the armed forces who has absolute authority). Peru's most recent military dictatorship ruled from 1968 to 1980. By 1979, a new constitution had been drawn up, and in 1980, Fernando Belaunde Terry won the presidency in Peru's first fully democratic election. Unfortunately, it would take more than a freely elected president to fix the economic problems that Peru was now facing after years of government instability and mismanagement.

Armed Opposition

Civilian rule failed to solve Peru's many problems. The government's response to terrorism led to many restrictions on civil liberties and freedoms. In addition, corruption continued to flourish in the executive, legislative, and judicial branches of government. Most important, poverty was as crushing as ever. In response to years of suffering under corrupt governments and a repressive military, two rebel groups formed with the purpose of defeating the ruling government in order to create a better society. They remain active today and continue to inflict terror on the nation's citizens.

One group was called the Shining Path and was an offshoot of the Peruvian Communist Party. Its members felt that anyone who was not on their side was actively fighting against them and was therefore an appropriate target for a violent attack. Members of the Shining Path have killed thousands of people over the years, many of whom were innocent civilians.

The other group was called the Tupac Amarú Revolutionary Movement, or MRTA. The MRTA was founded in 1983 by Victor Polay, Nestor Cerpa, and Miguel Rincon. These men had grown up in a repressive society that was dominated by the military. They wanted to create a political party that would help Peru become a better, freer, and fairer place to live. Originally, they had been members of the American Popular Revolutionary Alliance (APRA). They soon felt, however, that this political party was not working hard enough toward its goal of helping the poor and disenfranchised (those who are excluded from wealth, power, and the political process). Instead, they felt that the APRA party was focusing on helping people who were better off in order to gain their financial support and votes.

A mother and two of her children clear weeds from a plot of coca in Peru's Monzon Valley. Peru is the world's largest single source of coca leaves, providing about two-thirds of the total cocaine produced in the world. Coca cultivation was practiced by the ancient Andean Inca Empire. The Incas used coca for religious and medicinal purposes. In recent times, terrorist groups like the MRTA and Shining Path have used peasants to farm coca in an effort to fund their guerrilla activities.

Polay, Cerpa, and Rincon formed the MRTA because they wanted to get the attention of the Peruvian people, to reveal to them how corrupt their government was, and to explain what the MRTA was going to do to change things. Young MRTA members were told that they would be fighting for equality for millions of Peruvians. Inspired, many young Peruvians eagerly joined up.

Taking from the Rich and Giving to the Poor

In 1980, about half of the population of Peru lived in poverty. Millions of people lived in homes without electricity, running water, bathrooms, or enough food. The crops that they grew and sold did not earn them enough money to live on. The one crop that they could make a substantial profit on, coca, is illegal to grow because it is the plant from which cocaine is produced. Though very profitable, it is also a very risky crop. Coca fields are routinely destroyed by Peruvian and U.S. antinarcotic government agents.

The MRTA wanted to combat both the extreme poverty outside Peru's cities and the corrupt government in Lima. One of the group's first waves of attacks involved hijacking trucks that were delivering food to supermarkets in Lima. Armed with a few guns and a small amount of ammunition, MRTA members stole the food off the trucks and handed it out to the poor people in the area, like modern-day Robin Hoods. Not only did this allow the MRTA to feed a few hungry people, it was also a good way of creating good will and recruiting people to become members of the group.

A Ray of Hope Extinguished

In 1985, another democratic election took place, and Alan Garcia, a member of the APRA and a childhood friend of MRTA founder Victor Polay, became president. For the first time in Peru's history, there was a peaceful exchange of power from one democratically elected president to another. Peru seemed to be heading down a new road into a far brighter future.

Because President Garcia had been a friend of Victor Polay's and because the MRTA sought to work within the political system, the

Alan Garcia was elected president of Peru in 1985, riding a wave of optimism that greater social equality and good government would finally become a reality throughout the country. Five years later, however, he left office in disgrace amid economic chaos, guerrilla and drug-related violence, and corruption charges.

group put out a statement saying it would halt all attacks and give President Garcia the opportunity to run the government for the benefit of the poor. The MRTA's goal was not the destruction of social order and government institutions, but instead the creation of a broad popular movement to make the transition to a new, socialist society possible. They sought a so-called quiet revolution, not a bloody one.

Unfortunately, President Garcia's attempts to rebuild Peru only created greater poverty. By the end of his term, the economy deteriorated further and President Garcia's administration was found to be corrupt. The MRTA lost faith in his leadership and felt obliged to resume its attacks.

A New Kind of Terrorism

In late 1987, the MRTA took over the city of Juanjui (population: 20,000) by overpowering and locking up its entire police force. Once the officials were behind bars, the MRTA organized a town meeting in which the people were offered a rare opportunity to speak out about their needs and those of their city. After the meeting, the MRTA organized a soccer game and threw a big party.

Not wanting to miss an opportunity for good press, MRTA members invited a television news crew to film the party and later broadcast the footage nationwide. They did this to help the people of Juanjui and to show them and the rest of the country the kind of good things the group wanted to do for all Peruvians. Though some people were thankful for this new kind of "terrorism," it was not appreciated by the Peruvian government. President Garcia issued a state of emergency in the Juanjui region, and a military offensive quickly followed. As a result, many MRTA members were killed.

Moving to the City

In the mid-1980s, the MRTA and the Shining Path both began to strike targets in the city of Lima. Until this time, most terrorist violence took place in the countryside, not in the cities where the wealthy people lived. As the terrorists began to venture out of the hills and into residential areas, Lima's wealthy residents were suddenly being threatened. They wanted immediate action from their leaders.

The U.S. Embassy in Lima represented power and money, which the MRTA felt was at the root of Peru's problems. In an effort to protest against U.S. imperialism (the belief that the United States exerts economic and political control over other nations), the MRTA tried to launch an attack against the embassy. In November 1985, two cars filled with MRTA guerrillas drove past the U.S. Embassy firing automatic weapons at the building. Another MRTA vehicle stopped in front of the embassy and a guerrilla tossed two sticks of dynamite at the outer gate. None of the weapons actually struck the inside of the embassy, and only minor damage was done to the building's exterior. No one was harmed in the attack. After the assault, the MRTA got on a local radio station to claim responsibility for the attack and to spread the message that it was U.S. money and the political influence it bought that was doing harm to the Peruvian people.

A New President Gets Tough on Terrorism

In 1990, a relatively unknown professor named Alberto Fujimori won the presidential election based on his tough stance against terrorism and with the help of his closest adviser, Vladimiro Montesinos. Fujimori had the support of the U.S. government and assured the people of Lima that he would make their homes safe again. He promised to go to great lengths to rid the Peruvian capital of terrorism.

It was very difficult, however, for President Fujimori to put a quick halt to the terrorist activities that had been going on for

Attacking the United States

The MRTA has launched more anti-U.S. attacks than any other terrorist organization in Latin America. Some of these include:

- A 1984 small arms attack on the U.S. Embassy in Lima
- A 1985 bombing of the Lima offices of the Texaco Corporation
- An attempted 1985 attack on the U.S. Embassy in Lima
- A 1987 attack on the U.S. Consulate in Lima
- Repeated attacks using rockets, mortars, and car bombs on the U.S. ambassador's residence

ten years. The MRTA and the Shining Path had many members who could survive in the jungle and fight a long guerrilla war. Many politicians had widely differing views on how to solve the problems that Peru was facing, and many of these opinions contradicted those of Fujimori. So, in April 1992, President Fujimori chose to bypass Peru's new democratic system and instead dissolved the Congress, fired the judges who disagreed with him, and wrote a new constitution.

Fujimori now ruled the country as a dictator and created new antiterrorism laws and an antiterrorist police force known as the DINCOTE to speed the arrest of alleged terrorists. These new laws would not have been accepted by the Peruvian Congress because they denied people their basic civil rights. International human-rights groups say that these laws were designed to convict as many people as possible with very little evidence and to ensure they received very long prison sentences.

President Alberto Fujimori *(center)*, Interior Minister General Cesar Saucedo *(left)*, and Police Chief General Fernando Dianderas of Peru make the sign of the cross during a ceremony in a police station in Callao, Peru. A former agricultural economist, dean of the faculty of sciences at the Agrarian National University in La Molina, Peru, and talk-show host, Fujimori created a populist, grassroots political party called Cambio 90, which capitalized on popular anger and disappointment with Alan Garcia's administration. In the 1990 elections, Fujimori beat Garcia and famous author Mario Vargas Llosa to gain the presidency of Peru.

One of the new laws President Fujimori created was called the Repentance Law, which states that if you admit to being a member of a terrorist group and turn in other members (regardless of the truth of your accusation), you will be given more lenient treatment. The idea was to have terrorists turn in other terrorists in exchange

Government Terrorism

A little more than a year after President Fujimori's election, there was an attack on a neighborhood party in the area of Lima known as Barrios Altos. At 10:30 PM, two four-wheel-drive vans pulled up to the party and men carrying automatic weapons with silencers jumped out. They ordered everyone to lie down on the floor and then started shooting. Fifteen people, including a nine-year-old boy, were killed. Although blamed on antigovernment terrorists at the time, human-rights groups have long believed that the Barrios Altos massacre, as it is commonly known, was not committed by a terrorist group but instead by La Colina, a division of Peru's National Intelligence Service (SIN), who thought terrorists were present at the block party. Today, it is generally accepted as fact that La Colina was responsible for the massacre.

for lighter sentences. Unfortunately, the people who were turned in were often unjustly accused and entirely innocent of any crime. Frequently, an accused terrorist would tell the police what they wanted to hear, regardless of the truth, in order to receive leniency (better treatment and a shorter sentence). Fujimori would later admit that there were hundreds of innocent people in prison as a result of the Repentance Law. In essence, Fujimori was attempting to sweep away all opposition, regardless of the cost.

With very little remaining opposition, Fujimori gave the military emergency powers to launch an all-out war against the Shining Path and the MRTA. As a result, human-rights groups say there was a sharp rise in violations by the Peruvian military's special forces.

Early Strikes and Major Setbacks

In 1992, despite government claims to ease Peruvians' suffering and attempts by the Shining Path and the MRTA to bring about a more equal distribution of wealth, almost half of the population of Peru still lived below the poverty line.

Meanwhile, the government of Peru, the Shining Path, and the MRTA were fighting and killing one another in their competing attempts to gain control of the country. According to the *Washington Post*, 35,000 people were killed from 1980 to 1990 by state-sponsored terrorism (the Peruvian government) and guerrilla terrorism (Shining Path and MRTA). Amnesty International attributes 53 percent of the killing to the Peruvian government, 46 percent of the killing to the Shining Path, and 1 percent to the MRTA. It is estimated that the MRTA killed approximately 200 people from 1983 to the mid-1990s. The MRTA was always more interested in getting publicity than in killing people to achieve its goals.

Attacking U.S. Interests

By the mid-1980s, the MRTA was well known for its high-profile strikes, often against wealthy businesspeople and U.S. property. The group was also known to fight back against the police and the military, though not always successfully.

The U.S. Embassy was a favorite target. In April 1986, the MRTA filled a car with dynamite and parked it in front of the embassy. When the car exploded, it blew a hole in the concrete wall that was built to protect the embassy. No one was hurt, but the MRTA's anti-American statement was clear. On that very same day, a bomb exploded at a Kentucky Fried Chicken restaurant in Lima, injuring twelve people. The MRTA scattered pamphlets at the restaurant to let people know who was responsible for the bomb and what the group stood for.

On October 8, 1987, the MRTA planted bombs at the U.S. Consulate and the Bolivian Embassy. Group members said that the attacks were meant to commemorate the twentieth anniversary of the death of the Latin American revolutionary leader Che Guevara, a major inspiration to the MRTA. Once again, no one was physically injured at the U.S. Consulate or at the Bolivian Embassy.

The MRTA would often call its targets ahead of time to warn that a bomb had been placed and urge an evacuation. Typically, MRTA attacks were full of sound and fury, but resulted in few, if any, injuries. It was the symbolism of the attacks that was so potent—the destruction of vulnerable American property and interests.

A New Tactic: Kidnapping

In order to have any hope of inspiring Peruvians to join its cause, the MRTA needed both publicity and money. With its attacks against American interests, the group received plenty of attention from the press, which helped to get its anti-American message out to the public. Money was a much harder resource to acquire. Future terrorist operations had to be funded with the help of other criminal activities, such as kidnapping.

The MRTA was able to raise money through the kidnapping of business executives who worked for large, wealthy corporations. By early 1990, most businesspeople did not feel safe walking the streets of Lima. An executive from Coca-Cola was kidnapped on his way home from work. A few days later, a pharmaceutical executive was abducted right out of his bulletproof car. The ransoms were collected, and both men were returned relatively unharmed.

The MRTA continued to state that it did not support any project that was based on the random killing of innocent Peruvians. Its members' actions throughout the 1990s, however, would not always support these claims.

On September 11, 1992, the MRTA kidnapped mining executive David Ballón Vera in Lima. Once he was in MRTA custody, MRTA members contacted his family and demanded a ransom. Even though the family paid the ransom, he was not returned. In February 1993, more than five months after he had been kidnapped, Ballón's body was found with two bullet wounds in the head. It appeared that he had also been starved.

The murder of David Ballón Vera violated MRTA principles and is thought to have been carried out by members who did not obey their leaders. It is regarded among MRTA members not as a turning point—a new embrace of violence and murder—but as a regrettable low point in MRTA history.

Another Source of Income

In addition to kidnapping, the MRTA was able to raise money and build an arsenal of weapons by protecting coca farmers from the authorities. The MRTA would act as a security force in the coca fields, protecting the peasants who grew the coca and the traffickers who bought and sold it. In exchange, they received money and weapons from the traffickers. The Shining Path struck a similar deal with the drug lords.

A Movement Weakened by Arrests

With President Fujimori's new antiterrorist laws and antiterrorist police force in place, thousands of people were being arrested. Among them were MRTA leaders and members.

MRTA cofounder, Victor Polay, was arrested in 1989 (before Fujimori came into office) and was sentenced to life in prison at the Canto Grande Prison in Lima. While in prison, he and several other MRTA members dug a tunnel through which to escape. By July 1990, they had successfully completed digging a 275-foot-long passageway, beginning inside the prison and ending just outside its walls. Before dawn one July morning, Victor Polay and at least fifty other MRTA members escaped. Once the prison officials realized what had happened, the police began a house-to-house search for the fugitives throughout Lima, eventually detaining over 20,000 people.

In 1992, Victor Polay was found and arrested again, this time during Fujimori's antiterrorist regime and was sent to a prison at the El Callao Naval Base. At El Callao, he would spend the first eight years of his life sentence in a dark six-foot-square concrete box, from which he was allowed out only one hour each day.

By the mid-1990s, the MRTA was essentially defeated. Most MRTA members were either in prison or dead. The practical goals of those still free changed. Rather than waging war against

MRTA members stand and huddle in their prison cells within one of Peru's notorious prisons for convicted terrorists. By the mid-1990s, most MRTA members were either in prison or had been killed by government antiterrorist forces.

government corruption and American imperialism, their focus was now far narrower. MRTA members were now fighting the random arrest and imprisonment of innocent people. In addition, in calling attention to the human-rights abuses occurring in the nation's jails, they hoped to improve prison conditions and free imprisoned MRTA members.

A New Constitution

Seeking a new and stronger weapon with which to attack terrorists, President Fujimori rewrote the Peruvian constitution in April 1992, allowing him to combat terrorism without having to go through the proper checks and balances that ensure that innocent people are not convicted. These constitutional changes allowed suspects to be rounded up, held indefinitely, charged, and convicted based upon very little evidence (sometimes just upon an accusation made by another suspect trying to earn lenience). President Fujimori—and many Peruvian citizens—felt it was worth jailing some innocent people as long as the terrorists got convicted as well.

In addition to the Repentance Law, Fujimori also created a new judicial system for terrorists as well as new prison regulations designed specifically for convicted terrorists. In these new courts, the judge wore a hood to protect his or her identity for fear of reprisals from terrorist groups when members were convicted. This practice led some to question who was actually under those hoods, and if he or she was really qualified to conduct such a trial. Lawyers were allowed to meet with their clients only for a limited period, giving them very little time to prepare an informed defense.

The MRTA's Good Works

The MRTA was not only involved with bombings, kidnappings, and drug lords, but with other, more positive aspects of Peruvian life as well. When workers and peasants went on strike they could usually count on support from the MRTA. The MRTA also publicized the deteriorating human-rights situation in the Andean area of Peru called San Martin. In this area, there was a lot of violence and many killings by the Shining Path, the Peruvian military, and the DINCOTE (antiterrorist police force), as well as the antinarcotic police force.

According to human-rights groups, the Peruvian prison system is designed to slowly kill convicted terrorists. No terrorist prisoners are allowed visitors during the first year of their imprisonments. They are often allowed out of their cells for only half an hour per day and are fed a poor diet of mostly starch and water. Each cell contains two prisoners and one hole in the ground to be used as a toilet. All visits take place with a plastic window or meshed metal fence between inmate and visitor. Some of the terrorist prisons are located at a very high altitude where the air is thin and the temperature is cold. None of the terrorist prisons provide heat to the cells. The conditions of several Peruvian prisons do not meet the basic requirements of international human-rights groups, and Peru has been asked to close them.

By 1996, all of the founders of the MRTA (except Nestor Cerpa) and hundreds of its members were in prison. Everyone convicted of being a terrorist was sent to the jails set aside specifically for

Colonel Jorge Sarmiento of the Peruvian national police holds a copy of the MRTA's underground newspaper during a 1997 press conference. Both rebels and government counterterrorist forces attempt to win the hearts and minds of Peruvians through propaganda—ideas, facts, or claims deliberately spread to further one's own cause or damage the cause of an opponent.

radical political prisoners. Those who were convicted of being a founder of a terrorist group—such as the MRTA's Victor Polay and Miguel Rincon, and Abimael Guzman of the Shining Path— were put in solitary confinement.

Uninvited Guests

On the evening of December 17, 1996, in a wealthy suburb of Lima, the Japanese ambassador was holding a party to celebrate the birthday of Japan's emperor. All of Lima's elite attended the event, including judges from Peru's Supreme Court, retired members of Peru's military and police, business executives, and diplomats from around the world, including the United States. Even the president's brother, Pedro Fujimori, was present.

Not long after the American ambassador, Dennis Jett, left the party, the few remaining unimprisoned MRTA members pulled off a surprise attack that would finally get the whole world's attention. This stunning success would come at a steep price, however. The MRTA's biggest attack would also be its last.

Hostages for Prisoners

With the help of some strategically placed dynamite and several members disguised as waiters, fourteen MRTA rebels stormed the residence of Japan's ambassador. They immediately took more than 700 guests hostage and announced their demands to the president of Peru, Alberto Fujimori, who was supposed to have been in attendance at the party that night. A rain delay in President Fujimori's flight to Lima spared him from becoming a hostage himself.

The Japanese ambassador's residence in Lima, Peru, is seen from a nearby rooftop on January 7, 1997, during the MRTA hostage taking. The fourteen rebels initially took 700 of the ambassador's guests hostage during a party commemorating the Japanese emperor's birthday, but within hours began releasing many of the female, ill, and elderly captives. Seventy-four hostages would remain in the residence throughout the four-month ordeal. The MRTA's flag can be seen flying from the roof of the residence. In exchange for the release of the hostages, the rebels demanded the release of jailed MRTA members and better living conditions for the nation's poor.

The captors' primary demand was the release of 400 imprisoned MRTA members who were being held in the inhumane conditions of several Peruvian terrorist prisons. Nancy Gilvonio, the wife of MRTA leader Nestor Cerpa, was in the Yanamayo terrorist prison. Most of the imprisoned MRTA members had received lengthy

During the hostage crisis in the Japanese ambassador's residence in Lima, Peru, MRTA members regularly hung banners from the roof of the building in an attempt to make their case directly to the public in Peru and worldwide. The banner on the left reads, "MRTA—Mothers, wives, and children of our prisoners also wait for their freedom. Peace for all Peruvians." The second banner reads, "MRTA—Peru of today, 13 million in extreme poverty. Where is the progress?"

sentences—from thirty years to life in prison. A life sentence in Peru is exactly that, imprisonment for the rest of the prisoner's life with no opportunity for parole or early release. The fourteen MRTA rebels also wanted to receive safe passage with the freed prisoners to either the Dominican Republic or politically like-minded Cuba. Their overriding goal was to expose the conditions of Peruvian terrorist prisons to the rest of the world.

The Long Wait

Within hours of the takeover, the MRTA began releasing hostages. They freed the women, most of whom were the wives of diplomats and businessmen, though some were journalists and politicians. Among the women released were President Fujimori's mother and sister. They also freed the elderly and the ill. The rebels divided up the hostages into two different groups. The people they considered innocent were put on the first floor, and the people whom they considered their enemies were held on the second floor. Most of the people put on the second floor were associated with the Peruvian military or government.

During the next four months, the leader of the takeover, Nestor Cerpa, negotiated with the Peruvian government. The rebels slept in shifts in order to keep an eye on their hostages and placed booby traps throughout the residence, in doorways, and around the grounds to prevent the hostages from escaping or government troops from invading. They accepted the help of the Red Cross, which brought box lunches for the hostages and the rebels, who occasionally ate together.

The hostages passed the time playing card games, writing, and talking to each other. It did not take long, though, for a sense of

High Ideals and a Holiday Gesture

In late December, a week after the embassy takeover, the MRTA released more hostages as a Christmas gesture. The media interviewed some of these newly released hostages. One man quoted at the time by the *New York Times* said that their captors were "obviously professionals in what they do and believe in what they do deeply." A released Canadian businessman told the *New York Times* he spoke with his captor and got the impression that "one of their [the MRTA's] principal preoccupations is the extreme poverty of the country." This would be the last time the MRTA would release a large number of hostages. Over the following long weeks, a few more were released for health reasons. Seventy-two hostages would remain for the duration of the embassy takeover.

disappointment and despair to set in as they realized that the negotiations were going to take a long time. No one could imagine how long, however.

Just when it seemed as though negotiations were moving forward, the Peruvian government chose to end the hostage situation through violent rather than diplomatic means. Looking back, it is unclear if the government ever intended any outcome other than the complete elimination of the MRTA.

A Bloody Conclusion

On April 22, 1997, 126 days after the MRTA rebels took over the residence, 150 members of the Peruvian military's special forces began their rescue mission. At 3:30 PM, while the rebels played their daily indoor soccer game, a bomb exploded just below their

A Peruvian soldier peers out of a hole on the grounds of the residence of the Japanese ambassador in Lima, Peru. On April 22, 1997, soldiers stormed the residence using tunnels to gain entry in a successful attempt to surprise MRTA rebels and end the four-month-old hostage crisis. Inset: Peruvian police officers lift the dead body of a fallen MRTA rebel from the roof of the ambassador's residence.

feet. The military had dug a tunnel under the residence, having been told by one of the released hostages exactly where the captors played soccer every day. The sound of digging had been masked by the playing of extremely loud music, which the terrorists assumed was the government's attempt at psychological warfare.

Many of the rebel players were killed immediately by the blast. Moments later, another explosion occurred at the mansion's front door, blowing it open, while another explosion was ignited on the roof. The Peruvian special forces stormed the residence. The hostages had been given a warning by the Red Cross liaison ten minutes before the rescue effort began and were told where not to be.

Once the special forces stormed the embassy, the hostages were quickly brought out to safety. Some of the MRTA rebels tried to defend themselves against the special forces, but they were severely outnumbered and poorly armed; they were all killed. It was later reported that some rebels were shot after they had surrendered. There is growing evidence that the military had been given "shoot to kill" instructions, and that when rebels surrendered they were executed instead of arrested.

In a statement regarding the hostage situation, Amnesty International asked the Peruvian authorities "to act on the appalling fact that several hundred innocent prisoners who have been falsely accused of terrorism still languish in jail." Amnesty International condemned the MRTA takeover of the ambassador's residence, but it still supports the need to improve the inhumane conditions of Peru's terrorist prisons and the release of all innocents unjustly convicted under the nation's tough antiterrorist laws.

Lori Berenson

Despite the fact that the MRTA was passionately opposed to American influence in Peru, the group would receive more international attention thanks to an American woman than it could ever have gained through its own actions. While opinions differ on just how involved with the MRTA Lori Berenson was, there is no doubt that she has graphically illustrated the plight of Peru's political prisoners to a previously unaware American audience.

The Road to Peru

Lori Berenson grew up in New York City. She studied music in high school and attended college at the prestigious Massachusetts Institute of Technology (MIT), majoring in anthropology. In 1989, while a freshman at MIT, Berenson participated in a student exchange program with the University of Central America in El Salvador. There, she experienced firsthand the violence of that country's civil war. She was moved by the inequality she saw and decided to take a leave of absence from MIT so that she could do something to help.

Berenson eventually left college for good and moved to Nicaragua, where she lived and worked for two years assisting members of the Salvadoran refugee community. During this

4

Lori Berenson was born and raised in New York City. She was one of the relatively few females to attend the Massachusetts Institute of Technology (MIT). Her studies brought her to El Salvador in the late 1980s where she examined the problem of unfair income and land distribution. In 1990, she traveled to Nicaragua to work among El Salvadoran refugees displaced by the civil war in their country. She traveled to Peru in November 1994 and became intrigued with the country's history, culture, and politics.

time, she also worked as a secretary, computer programmer, and translator for Salvadoran rebels living in exile in Nicaragua. After a peace treaty was signed between the Salvadoran government and the rebels, ending the twelve-year civil war,

Berenson moved to San Salvador (the capital of El Salvador) and spent two years working for one of the developing democracy's newly elected politicians. As she learned more about Latin America, Berenson became interested in Peru.

An Acquaintance with Terrorists

Berenson began her trip to South America in the fall of 1994, when she was twenty-five years old. As a student of anthropology, she enjoyed learning about different cultures. By December 1994, she had decided to live in Lima. She acquired journalist credentials from two small New York–based magazines so that she could write about the fate of women in Peru as well as other human-rights issues.

Once in Lima, Berenson became friends with a Panamanian architect, and together they rented a house in the La Molina area of that city. It was a large house, which the architect also used as a studio for his paintings. Berenson spent most of her time enjoying Lima and other parts of Peru, immersing herself in all aspects of Peruvian culture.

To offset some of the costs of the house, they sublet the fourth-floor apartment to someone who claimed to be an engineer. (He was actually Miguel Rincon, one of the founders of the MRTA. Berenson claims to have been unaware of his identity.) The engineer had houseguests staying with him from time to time. After a few months, Berenson claims that she wanted more privacy than the house provided, so she moved to an apartment in another neighborhood, San Borjia, closer to central Lima. Berenson was on her way back to this apartment from the congressional building where she worked when she was arrested.

The Arrest and Raid

On the evening of November 30, 1995, Lori Berenson and her friend Rosa were riding a Lima city bus on their way home from attending a session of Congress. As the bus came to a stop, two unmarked policemen climbed aboard the bus, dragged them off, and arrested them both. Berenson had been doing research for an article she was writing about poverty and women in Peru, and claimed that she had no idea why the Peruvian antiterrorism police (DINCOTE) were arresting her. Neither, it seemed, did Rosa. Berenson would later allege that her friend Rosa, who presented herself as a photographer from Bolivia, was actually Nancy Gilvonio, the wife of MRTA cofounder Nestor Cerpa and an alleged high-ranking MRTA member herself.

They were taken to the DINCOTE headquarters and questioned. A few hours later, Berenson was put into a car with fully armed DINCOTE officers and driven to the house in the La Molina neighborhood of Lima where she once lived. When they pulled up to the house, Berenson could see hundreds of armed soldiers surrounding the area. The police told her to go to the front door and ring the bell. She was very hesitant to follow their orders because there was obviously going to be a gunfight, and she knew there were children in nearby houses. Berenson said she would not get out of the car.

Instead, the DINCOTE stormed the house in search of MRTA rebels. Some of the rebels fired back. Others fled the house, went to a neighbor's home, and took the residents—three children, their mother, and a grandmother—hostage. With Berenson held in the car, the MRTA and the police fought through the night. By morning, three MRTA rebels and one policeman were dead. After negotiating

Lori Berenson, guarded by two police officers, enters a house used as a rebel hideout during a judicial investigation two weeks after her arrest by Peruvian security forces on November 30, 1995. Before her arrest, the New York City native had lived in a house in a Lima suburb shared by MRTA members. Berenson claims she was in the country working as a freelance journalist and that she never knew her housemates were suspected terrorists.

with a local priest, Miguel Rincon released the hostages from the neighbor's home and gave himself up as a prisoner of war.

The DINCOTE police arrested sixteen members of the MRTA who had been living at the house and found a large supply of weapons and ammunition. They also found floor plans and a three-dimensional model of the Peruvian Congress. The MRTA rebels were accused of planning an attack on the government building during which they were going to kidnap several congressional representatives, whom they would free in exchange for the release of imprisoned MRTA members. Berenson was included in the arrest, accused of being an MRTA leader and a participant in the planning of the attack on Congress.

Interrogation and Trial

Berenson was again interrogated when she was returned to the DINCOTE headquarters after the La Molina arrests and pressured to repent. During the following days, she was held in a cell at the headquarters and was told that others had repented and implicated her as a leader of the MRTA. Thanks to the investigative research of respected groups such as Amnesty International, it is widely known that the DINCOTE uses torture and the threat of torture to get people to confess or repent, though this did not work on Berenson. She told her interrogators that she was not currently and had never been a member of the MRTA, let alone one of its leaders.

Berenson was very quickly given a military (as opposed to a civil) trial, which, according to the antiterrorist laws of Fujimori's new constitution, is the appropriate court for people being tried on high-level terrorism charges. The rules for a military trial in Peru are different than those of a regular civil trial; the defendant does not get much time to speak to his or her lawyer, the judge wears a hood, and the prosecutor does not always tell the defendant what the charges are. There is no trial as we would understand it, with evidence presented by both sides and a jury of regular citizens deciding whether a person is guilty or not based upon this evidence. There is also no opportunity for cross-examination (when a defendant's lawyer can question prosecution witnesses and accusers). These trial conditions are condemned by international human-rights and legal organizations because it makes it impossible for accused people to properly defend themselves. As a result, the conviction rate of people tried in the military courts is almost 100 percent, unless they repent.

Berenson's "trial" violated international standards of justice to an even greater degree than Peru's typical military terrorist trials. Rather than taking place in a courtroom with a judge and jury, her trial more closely resembled a series of conferences between the judge, the prosecutor, and the defense attorney. The prosecutor claimed that Berenson was a leader of the MRTA and a traitor to Peru (despite the fact that she's an American—not a Peruvian citizen). Her lawyer did his best to defend her, but he let Berenson and her parents, Mark and Rhoda, know that he would have a difficult time proving her innocence given the restrictions placed upon him. During the trial period, Berenson was held at the DINCOTE headquarters and was able to see her parents almost every day.

The Conviction and Sentence

As predicted by her lawyer, Berenson was quickly found guilty of being a leader of the MRTA and a traitor to Peru. While awaiting her sentence, she was moved to a cell in the prison across the street from the DINCOTE headquarters. Even after her conviction, she was interrogated at all hours of the day and night and was occasionally denied bathroom privileges. Two weeks before her sentence was handed down, she was forced to share her filthy, rat-infested cell with a woman who had just had surgery and was suffering from injuries that no one was tending to.

Lori Berenson began serving the life sentence handed down to her by a Peruvian military tribunal at Yanamayo Prison (pictured here), 525 miles southeast of Lima, and 12,700 feet above sea level, high in the Andes. The prison is said to be so cold that inmates' hands turn purple when they wash their own clothing (as they are required to do). Following the overturning of the life sentence and a new conviction in a civil court, Berenson was moved to Socabaya Prison outside Arequipa, Peru, to begin a twenty-year sentence.

After ten days of this treatment, sleep deprived and emotionally unstable, she was told that she would be presented to the media and given sixty seconds to tell her side of the story. Following almost two weeks of sleepless nights shared with an injured and helpless woman, Berenson suddenly found herself thrust into a room filled with television cameras, all pointing at her. She looked disheveled and spoke in a very loud and angry voice. She had been told to yell because there was no microphone. Berenson seemed out of control. Her parents said they had never seen her like this before. They wondered what must have been done to her in prison to make her look and sound this way. In her presentation, Berenson spoke about the hunger, misery, and injustice that exists in Peru and said that the MRTA are not terrorists, but revolutionaries. She said she loves the people of Peru and is confident that someday there will be justice for all Peruvians.

Under usual circumstances, once prisoners are convicted of terrorism and sentenced, they are then presented to the press, giving them one last opportunity to speak before being taken off to prison. This way, a prisoner's final statement cannot be used against him or her when determining a prison sentence. Berenson, however, was presented to the media before her sentencing. As a result of her speech, the thirty-year sentence that was requested by the prosecution was reconsidered, and the judge gave her a life sentence instead.

In Yanamayo

Berenson was quickly sent to the infamous Yanamayo terrorist prison, located in the Andes at 12,700 feet above sea level. In this remote, frigid location, she would begin serving her life sentence. At Yanamayo, there is no heating, the cells are six feet by ten feet long, the walls and the beds are made of concrete, and there is a hole in the floor that serves as a toilet. Across from Berenson's cell, there is a small window close to the ceiling with bars but no glass. The window lets in a little light and a lot of cold. Two inmates share each cell and sleep on the concrete slabs. The inmates are allowed out of their cold cells for only half an hour each day.

Peruvian police guard the Lima house where Lori Berenson allegedly helped MRTA members plot an attack on the Peruvian Congress in 1995. During Berenson's civil retrial on terrorism charges, she was brought back to her old home for a re-enactment of events surrounding her arrest. Berenson continues to insist that she never met the MRTA rebels living upstairs from her and certainly never knew they were members of a terrorist organization.

Berenson was not allowed visitors during her first year in prison. Her parents flew to Yanamayo from New York City as soon as they heard she had been sentenced and were surprised and deeply disappointed to find out that they could not see their daughter. They were, however, allowed to leave some sweaters and toiletries for her.

Lori Berenson: In Her Own Words

When asked by the author how she would describe her situation, Lori Berenson, currently serving her sentence at the Huacariz Prison in Cajamarca, Peru, had this to say:

"My situation [is the same as] that of thousands of Peruvians (and millions of human beings on Earth). I am currently imprisoned for my belief in and work for social justice. Although being in prison is extremely difficult, much worse than that would be renouncing my principles or becoming an accomplice to a system of injustice."

Berenson's parents would travel from New York City to visit her as often as was allowed, usually twice a month for one hour. They brought food, clothes, vitamins, and medicine for Berenson, who shared them with her fellow inmates. Without these gifts, it is unlikely Berenson would have been able to stay healthy in the harsh living conditions of Yanamayo.

A New Trial

In 2000, after spending five years in Peruvian terrorist prisons, Berenson's conviction was overturned when some politicians, who had been held at the Japanese ambassador's residence during the hostage crisis, publicly offered proof that she was not a leader of the MRTA. She was given a new trial, this one in a civilian (as opposed to a military) terrorism court. Peru's civil terrorist courts have three judges (who do not wear hoods) but no jury. Berenson's parents continue to visit her in prison a minimum of once a month.

Lori Berenson's parents attend the retrial of their daughter on April 4, 2001, in civil court. The trial would result in a conviction and a twenty-year jail term. Berenson's parents continue to wage a public-relations battle on their daughter's behalf, lobbying members of the U.S. Congress, the Inter-American Human Rights Commission, and the Organization of American States.

In the summer of 2001, Berenson was found guilty by this civil court of being a collaborator (defined as having befriended an MRTA member, regardless of whether or not she was aware that the person was a member of the group) and sentenced to twenty years in prison. According to the U.S. State Department, Peru's civilian terrorism court has failed "to meet international standards of openness, fairness, and due process." Human-rights groups around the world condemn Peru's terrorism courts—both civil and military—and the antiterrorism laws. Many have said that it is impossible for Lori Berenson to find justice in Peru. Amnesty International considers her a political prisoner.

Berenson appealed her conviction as a collaborator, but her request was denied in February 2002. Unless the new president of Peru, Alejandro Toledo, or a future successor pardons her or grants her clemency (a reduced sentence), or the controversial antiterrorist laws in Peru change, Lori Berenson will be released from prison on November 29, 2015. She will be forty-six years old.

Her chances of an early release do not seem promising. On March 25, 2002, according to the Associated Press, President Toledo told U.S. president George W. Bush, who had suggested clemency for her, that the issue of Lori Berenson is "totally closed."

Conclusion

Even as the MRTA died, the government it sought to replace began to unravel, sinking under the weight of the crimes MRTA members had long sought to expose. In the midst of a widening scandal involving government corruption and human-rights abuses, Fujimori resigned as president in November 2001 and fled to Japan, the country where his parents were born. There is also reason to believe that Fujimori himself was born in Japan, a fact he hid in order to be eligible to run for the presidency of Peru. Japan quickly gave him citizenship, and as a result, he cannot be extradited (sent back) to Peru to face the charges against him. Japanese law does not allow extradition of its citizens.

Proof of the corruption that the MRTA long claimed was present within the Fujimori government emerged in 2000 when video-tapes turned up that showed Vladimiro Montesinos (head of Peru's National Intelligence Service and a close adviser to the president) bribing judges and politicians. Montesinos is currently being investigated on charges of arms and drug trafficking and illegal money transfers. He was also found to possess several Swiss bank accounts containing more than $100 million dollars, most of it probably stolen from the government treasury, while millions of Peruvian citizens continued to live in utter poverty.

Since his flight to Japan, Fujimori has been indicted on crimes linking him and Montesinos to the death squads responsible for the

The grave of Nestor Cerpa, military leader and cofounder of the MRTA, stands alone in a corner of Nueva Esperanza Cemetery in the Villa Maria section of Lima, Peru. Cerpa and thirteen other MRTA members were killed by antiterrorist commandos when the Peruvian government put an end to the MRTA's takeover of the Japanese ambassador's residence in Lima. The government buried the fourteen dead MRTA rebels in various graveyards in shantytowns on the outskirts of Lima, without any funeral services. The families of the dead MRTA members had wanted to give them Christian burials, but their requests were denied.

Barrios Altos massacre. Following the capture of Montesinos in 2001, the existence of state-sponsored terrorism has been proven, supporting what human-rights groups have said for years—that thousands of innocent people were killed at the hands of the Peruvian government's special forces.

In 2000, Alejandro Toledo was elected as the new president of Peru. In the previous election, he had come in second to Fujimori, but that earlier race was later declared unfair. President Toledo has said that his administration's first priority will be reducing poverty. The Peruvian people have heard the exact same words from previous presidents and are understandably skeptical. In 2002, approximately half the Peruvian population continued to live in poverty.

On the human-rights and democracy fronts, the new president is not doing any better. President Toledo has yet to restore the 1979 constitution abolished by Fujimori and undo the illegal imprisonments brought about by the Fujimori government's antiterrorism laws. Nor has he closed any of the terrorist prisons deemed unacceptable by international human-rights groups.

Following the release of a forensic report in May 2002 that showed that eight of the MRTA members killed in the ambassador's residence had been shot execution-style in the base of the neck, Peruvian prosecutor Richard Saavedra filed homicide charges against eighteen army officers and Montesinos. Fujimori's role in the executions is also being investigated. In July 2002, Montesinos was convicted of abuse of authority and sentenced to nine years in prison.

The MRTA was never a very large group. In the late 1980s, at the height of its popularity, it had no more than 2,000 operatives. Membership began to fall after the 1992 arrest of Victor Polay. In October 1993, over 100 mid-level members of the MRTA surrendered to the Peruvian security forces under the guidelines of President Fujimori's Repentance Law. The La Molina shootout and arrests decreased the number of high-ranking members even further.

The MRTA tried to make a comeback with the 1996 takeover of the Japanese ambassador's residence by gaining the release of

In this still image taken from a surveillance videotape, former Peruvian spy chief Vladimiro Montesinos *(right)* hands over money to the president of Panamericana Television (Channel 5 in Lima), Ernesto Schutz, in 1998. This bribe was paid in exchange for Channel 5's support for the government of then-president Alberto Fujimori and his reelection campaign. This is exactly the sort of government corruption and misuse of public funds the MRTA sought to expose and publicize before the group's ranks were depleted by arrests and deaths.

its imprisoned comrades and generating a new wave of publicity for its cause. Instead, the group was all but buried.

The MRTA is now thought to have no more than 100 active members, mostly young fighters who lack leadership skills and experience. Over the years, the group's focus has shifted from revolutionary activity to attempts to free imprisoned MRTA members. The group has not pulled off any major terrorist attacks since the takeover of the ambassador's residence, and in 2001, it was removed from the U.S. State Department's list of foreign terrorist organizations.

The MRTA emerged from Peru's impoverished villages to fight for economic and political justice for all Peruvians. Because of its members' commitment to the well-being of their fellow citizens, they sought to avoid harming the innocent in their attacks upon the symbols of all that they thought was destroying Peru. According to MRTA founder Victor Polay, the MRTA sometimes used violence to achieve its goals of social change but never rejected political dialogue that could have avoided civil war. Ultimately, the MRTA failed to bring about the social and political changes it wanted.

The MRTA's relatively bloodless actions did indeed call attention to government corruption and human-rights abuses. Perhaps whatever improvements occur in Peruvian society as a result of this new awareness can be attributed at least in part to the MRTA's efforts. Nearly all of the group's members sacrificed themselves to their ideals, ending up either in prison or dead. A group that tried—and sometimes failed—to avoid bloodshed was itself destroyed by the kind of government-sponsored violence it was seeking to expose. Perhaps the MRTA's message was never more clearly illustrated than it was in the group's violent death.

Glossary

ambassador A high-ranking diplomatic official, appointed by his or her government as its representative to a host country. The ambassador lives and works in the host country.

Andes The principal mountains of Peru with peaks that rise higher than 20,000 feet above sea level and that run along the western edge of South America.

DINCOTE (Counter-Terrorism National Directorate) Peruvian antiterrorist police force that was created by the Fujimori government specifically to fight terrorism.

diplomat A person who deals with international relations, negotiating treaties, alliances, and agreements between countries.

imperialism When powerful nations try to control or influence weaker ones. The United States is accused of practicing these policies.

Inca Empire In the fifteenth century, the Incas built a wealthy and complex empire of over nine million people in the Andes. The Spanish conquered the Inca Empire in the early sixteenth century.

Incas Native South American people whose empire flourished from about AD 1438 to the arrival of the Spanish in AD 1532. The descendants of the Incas account for roughly 50 percent of today's population of Peru.

revolutionary Somebody who is committed to causing, supporting, or advocating a political or social change; someone fighting for the overthrow of a government and the installation of a new system of rule.

SIN (National Intelligence Service) The Peruvian government's national intelligence service that was led by Vladimiro Montesinos during President Fujimori's term in office.

terrorist A person who uses terror, violence, and intimidation to create a state of fear to achieve a political or social goal.

Yanamayo One of Peru's terrorist prisons, located at 12,700 feet above sea level in the northern town of Puno Peru. Lori Berenson spent the first three years of her sentence there.

For More Information

Amnesty International
322 Eighth Avenue
New York, NY 10001
(212) 807-8400
Web site: http://www.amnesty.org

Central Intelligence Agency (CIA)
Office of Public Affairs
Washington, DC 20505
(703) 482-0623
Web site: http://www.cia.gov

Centre for the Study of Terrorism and Political Violence
Department of International Relations
University of St. Andrews
St. Andrews, Scotland KY16 9AL
Web site: http://www.st-and.ac.uk/academic/intrel/research/cstpv

Federation of American Scientists (FAS)
Intelligence Resource Program
1717 K Street NW
Suite 209
Washington, DC 20036
(202) 454-4691
Web site: http://www.fas.org/irp/index.html

Human Rights Watch
350 Fifth Avenue
34th Floor
New York, NY 10118-3299
(212) 290-4700
Web site: http://www.hrw.org

National Security Agency (NSA)
Public Affairs Office
9800 Savage Road
Fort George G. Meade, MD 20755-6779
(301) 688-6524
Web site: http://www.nsa.gov

National Security Institute (NSI)
116 Main Street
Suite 200
Medway, MA 02053
(508) 533-9099
Web site: http://nsi.org

Terrorist Group Profiles
Dudley Knox Library
Naval Post Graduate School
411 Dyer Road
Monterey, CA 93943
Web site: http://web.nps.navy.mil/~library/tgp/tgp2.htm

For More Information

Washington Office on Latin America
1630 Connecticut Avenue NW
Suite 200
Washington, DC 20009
(202) 797-2171
Web site: http://www.wola.org

Web Sites

Due to the changing nature of Internet links, the Rosen
Publishing Group, Inc., has developed an online list of Web sites
related to the subject of this book. This site is updated regularly.
Please use this link to access the list:

http://www.rosenlinks.com/iwmito/pemr/

For Further Reading

Berenson, Rhoda. *Lori: My Daughter Wrongfully Imprisoned in Peru*. New York: Context Books, 2000.

Everts, Tammy. *Peru: The People and Culture*. Minneapolis, MN: Econo-Clad Books, 1999.

Kalman, Bobbie. *Peru: The Land*. New York: Crabtree Publishing Co., 1994.

King, David C. *Peru: Lost Cities, Found Hopes*. Boston: Benchmark Books, 1997.

Landau, Elaine. *Peru*. New York: Children's Press, 2000.

MacDonald, Fiona, and David Salariya. *Inca Town*. New York: Franklin Watts, Inc., 1999.

Poole, Deborah, and Gerardo Renique. *Peru: Time of Fear*. London: Latin America Bureau, 1992.

Worth, Richard. *Pizarro and the Conquest of the Incan Empire in World History*. Berkeley Heights, NJ: Enslow Publishers, Inc., 2000.

Bibliography

Associated Press. "Berenson Case Is Closed, Bush Hears in Peru." *New York Times*, March 26, 2002.

Associated Press. "Fujimori Is Charged in Death Squad Murders." *New York Times*, September 6, 2001.

Associated Press. "Peruvian Rebel Refuses to Repent." *New York Times*, March 7, 2002.

Berenson, Lori, written reply to author's questions, April 2, 2002.

Berenson, Mark, interview with author, New York, NY, March 29, 2002.

Berenson, Rhoda, interview with author, New York, NY, March 29, 2002.

Berenson, Rhoda. *Lori: My Daughter Wrongfully Imprisoned in Peru*. New York: Context Books, 2000.

Bridges, Tyler. "Peru's New President Vows to Lift Nation from Poverty." *Miami Herald*, July 29, 2001.

Brooke, James. "The Rebels and the Cause: 12 Years of Peru's Turmoil." *New York Times*, December 19, 1996.

Escobar, Gabriel. "Peru Rebels More Agile at Delivering Message Abroad than at Home." *Washington Post*, January 19, 1997.

Forero, Juan. "Prisoners in Peru Seek a Way Out; Captives of War Demand New Trials." *New York Times*, March 30, 2002.

Hilton, Isabel. "The Government Is Missing; Fujimori and Montesinos Vanished Amid Strange Stories of Soothsayers,

Bribes, and Secret Videos. But Who Was Really in Charge?" *The New Yorker*, March 5, 2001.

Krauss, Clifford. "Released Hostages Say Rebels Acted with Restraint." *New York Times*, December 24, 1996.

Krauss, Clifford. "Rescue in Peru: The Overview; Peru Troops Rescue Hostages; Rebels Slain as Standoff Ends." *New York Times,* April 23, 1997.

Poole, Deborah, and Gerardo Rénique. *Peru: Time of Fear*. London: Latin America Bureau, 1992.

Reyes, Francisco. "Peru's Deadly Drug Habit: Behind the Fujimori Front, Corruption and Cocaine Trafficking Are Booming." *Washington Post*, February 28, 1993.

Robinson, Eugene. "Amid Peru's Ills, Justice System Heads the List; New President Outraged by Prison Conditions." *Washington Post*, August 4, 1990.

Rudolph, James D. *Peru: The Evolution of a Crisis*. Westport, CT: Praeger Publishers, 1992.

Sheridan, Mary Beth. "Peruvian Prison Life Is Backdrop to Hostage Crisis." *Los Angeles Times*, December 27, 1996.

Simpson, John. *In the Forests of the Night: Encounters in Peru with Terrorism, Drug-Running, and Military Oppression*. New York: Random House, 1994.

Stavig, Ward. *The World of Tupac Amarú: Conflict, Community, and Identity in Colonial Peru*. Lincoln, NE: University of Nebraska Press, 1999.

Strong, Simon. *Shining Path: Terror and Revolution in Peru*. New York: Times Books, 1993.

Index

About the Author

Suzie Baer is an independent filmmaker who lives with her husband and son in New York City.

Photo Credits

Cover, pp. 32–33 © Fernando Llano/AP/Wide World Photos; p. 1 © Luis Romero/AP/Wide World Photos; pp. 5, 6, 10, 42, 51 © AP/Wide World Photos; pp. 12, 25, 49 © Martin Mejia/AP/Wide World Photos; pp. 16, 44, 46 © Corbis; p. 22 © Fotos De MRTA; pp. 27, 28–29 © Scott Dalton/AP/Wide World Photos; p. 28 (inset) © Douglas Engle/AP/Wide World Photos; p. 33 (inset) © Ricardo Mazalan/AP/Wide World Photos; p. 36 © Mark and Rhoda Berenson; p. 39 © Silvia Izquierdo/AP/Wide World Photos.

Series Design and Layout

Nelson Sá